Abundant Light

DR. CYNTHIA JACKSON SMALL

and Co-Author

JESSICA LOREN SMALL

ISBN 978-1-0980-8429-5 (paperback)
ISBN 978-1-0980-8430-1 (digital)

Christian Faith Publishing, Inc.
832 Park Avenue
Meadville, PA 16335
www.christianfaithpublishing.com

Printed in the United States of America

To William and Beanna Jackson,
godly parents, grandparents, and role models who are
celebrated as beacons of abundant light in our family.

You are the light of the
world. A town built on a
hill cannot be hidden.
                    —Matthew 5:14

CONTENTS

INTRODUCTION

Abundant Light is an inspirational book that is designed to shed light into the darkness that surrounds us in these perilous times. Our Father has given us the assignment to share stories and examples of a Savior who is ever present in the times of trouble, an anchor in times of life's emergencies, and the navigator who can lead us safely through any storm. We are excited to introduce a Savior who is the King of Kings, Lord of Lords, one who has all power in His hands, and can do anything but fail. Although many know Him based on what they have read or heard, we are delighted to share the Father based on our personal relationship and experiences living in His daily presence. Jessica and I invite you to travel with us on a learning journey to take a closer look at our Savior who is the light of the world (John 8:12).

As you read the following chapters, we hope to share rays of hope and encouragement that will brighten your daily walk with the Lord. With this in mind, Jessica and I have teamed up to share our personal testimonies that clearly illustrate God's light that appeared during dark days in our lives. Through our trials, challenges, and bumps in the road, we can now see how God turned darkness into light and brought peace in the midst of storms. Yes, there have been some rough roads along life's journey, but the Word of God reminded us to look beyond our problems and focus on God's promises.

Essentially, we have both learned from our individual experiences that in order to arrive at our destinations in life, we must follow and walk in God's abundant light.

We are delighted to be used as instruments of God to share messages that will allow you to see a glimpse of hope even in seasons of darkness. Our prayer is that readers of all ages will be inspired to let their light shine so that others may see Jesus and glorify our Father in heaven (Matthew 5:16). As we live in the Word of God and allow the Word to shine in our lives, we will become reflections of light that will draw men to Christ.

Just imagine a world that is filled with witnesses who let their light shine in all four corners of the earth each day. With this kind of light source, we can create worldwide lighthouses that reflect rays of healing, peace, joy, hope, and deliverance in the midst of life's storms. As Bible believers, may we reflect light through our smiles, tears, conversations, and actions so that others will see God's abundant light at work in us. Further, we pray that the love of Christ shines from within so that others will not focus on our clothing but on the beauty of God's Word that resides in our heart (1 Peter 3:4).

We sincerely hope that you will find our testimonies and stories meaningful as you begin or continue your journey with the Father. And whatever you may be going through in life, we hope that you will find sources of light from this book that will brighten your pathway as you travel on this earthly highway. Please know that our primary purpose for being transparent in sharing our personal stories is to allow you to see how God changed some of our darkest days into life-changing experiences through His marvelous light.

Prepare now to receive what God has given us to give you—reflections of His abundant light that yet shines throughout the world and within those who walk daily in His image. Shine on for His glory!

Chapter 1

I AM THE LIGHT

When Jesus spoke again to the people,
he said, "I am the light of the world.
Whoever follows me will never walk in
darkness, but will have the light of life."
—John 8:12

The light of the Lord is a brilliant and powerful projection of God's glory even in a dark world. His light is everlasting and never changes. This abundant source of light cannot be extinguished or suppressed, and neither can it be turned on or off. Batteries are not needed to illuminate this special light, and it is not available in any store. Believers have discovered this supernatural light after accepting the Lord as their personal Savior. Once received, the light takes residence in the hearts of individuals who follow and reflect this glorious light. The light I refer to is Jesus Christ who is the light of the world.

As I have experienced different challenges in life, I have learned to walk in the abundant and never-ending light of our Savior. Looking through a spiritual lens today, I can see this miraculous light in times of sickness, pain, sorrow, and other seasons of afflictions in life. I know from personal experiences that Jesus yet reigns as the balm in Gilead and has supernatural power to heal all manner of illnesses and diseases. I am reminded through God's Word that many are the afflictions of the righteous, but the Lord delivers us out of them all (Psalm 34:19).

I often reflect on times when I have witnessed the miraculous power of a Savior who showed up on the scene and brought healing in the room. When I think of God's goodness and healing power, I rejoice in knowing that the Father is faithful and attentive to our needs. What a joy it is to experience the wonder-working touch of God who can heal, deliver, and set us free. From many personal experiences, I have learned the importance of sharing special stories of God's healing power that turned tests into testimonies and problems into praises. It is such a blessing to know that we overcome by the words of our testimony (Revelations 12:11).

With this in mind, I'd like to share a testimony about my mom who became very ill and experienced numerous visits to the hospital in her eighties. I recall a time in particular when Mom had difficulty breathing and was rushed by ambulance to the hospital. In the emergency room, doctors and nurses worked diligently to spare Mom's life from a congenital heart condition. As my brothers and sister waited to hear an update from the doctors, we began to pray and call on the name of the Lord.

After stabilizing Mom's blood pressure, the doctors shared their prognosis and next steps which did not sound very promising. I remember one of the doctors saying to our family, "We will monitor your mom's condition in the intensive care unit since she has gone through a traumatic experience." We were also told that Mom had been sedated and that she may not recognize us or be able to communicate when she awakens. Despite this report, I kept trusting God and believing for the best outcome. Through this and other challenging experiences, I learned to stand on God's promises and believe the report of the Lord.

While waiting for Mom to wake up, my siblings and I decided that we would take shifts and remain with her day and night. As I was sitting with Mom one night, I began to read the Bible and meditate on His Word. Then I heard the voice of the Lord say, *The doctors have done their work, now it's time for you to do my work.* I immediately looked inside my purse for a small vial of oil that I carried with me daily. In obedience to God, I anointed Mom's head with oil and began to pray for her complete healing. Mom slept peacefully through the night.

Fast forward to the next evening, I returned to sit with Mom around 6:00 p.m. My brother who had been with Mom all morning said that she had not awakened during his shift. While sitting in a chair next to Mom's bed, I began to read the Word. About a half hour later, Mom woke up. She opened her eyes and looked at me with a smile on her face. Before I could say anything to Mom, she spoke to me saying, "Hi, Cynthia, ain't it a wonder about Jesus!" I am sure you can imagine the joy I felt when I heard these powerful words. Not only did Mom recognize and call me by name, she also let me know that God had touched her body. "Thank you Jesus" is all I could say as I rejoiced with tears of joy.

Certainly the presence of the Lord was in the room. This was definitely the result of God's powerful light that projected victory over death for my mom. What I understand now is that the report from the doctors was overruled by God's amazing healing power. Further, I know that the enemy had plans to kill, steal, and destroy Mom's life; but almighty God said, "Not so." Praise God for His abundant light that arrived just in time to declare life and that more abundantly (John 10:10).

I called the nurse to let her know Mom was awake. Nurses and doctors quickly came to check Mom's vital signs. They began to remove tubes and other medical equipment. One of the doctors began to call Mom the "miracle lady" as her health and strength was miraculously restored. He even wrote this comment on Mom's medical chart. God indeed smiled on Mom and delivered her from a dark season through His abundant light. I am happy to report that Mom was released from the hospital in just a few days with a victorious testimony of divine healing. To God be the glory!

As I look back over my life, I can recall many other experiences that reflect the power of God's light in my life. I must share a personal story regarding a time when I needed a breakthrough. I share this experience openly so that hopefully it will be a blessing to someone who may be going through a stressful season in life.

In 2019, I recall driving to work one Friday morning feeling tired, exhausted, and at a point of throwing in the towel. I felt drained of energy, overwhelmed, and overloaded with many tasks. Although this particular day began with clear skies and lots of sunshine, I really dreaded going to work. I felt a heavy cloud over me and wanted to return home and crawl back into the bed. Yet I continued to drive to work in the midst of what felt like a dark day of despair.

I recall stopping at a red light and hearing the Holy Spirit say, *Look up to your left.* I immediately obeyed and saw the sun. It was so bright that it was difficult to look at it without sunglasses. Then I heard the Spirit declare these words, *Arise and shine, for your light has come and my glory arises upon you.* At that moment I began to feel the presence of the Lord and responded with tears in my eyes, *Yes, Lord.* I knew then that the Lord was preparing a way of escape for me. In my heart, I knew that God would allow me to rise in His abundant light that reflects peace in times of stressful seasons.

When the Lord speaks, you can expect things to change. A few months later, the Lord allowed me to retire after serving children and families for thirty-five years. When I was given this directive to retire, a weight was immediately lifted from my shoulders. I could not wait to shout once the retirement was finalized, so I rejoiced and praised God in advance. One of my favorite quotes that is so powerful is a message from Vivian Greene who shares: "Life isn't about waiting for the storm to pass. It's about learning how to dance in the rain."

With that said, no matter what you are facing in life, it's a great time to put on your dancing shoes and dance in the midst of the storm!

I praise God for allowing me to retire a month later with benefits and less stress in my life. I discovered that God had smiled on me and was shining in my life, family, finances, and in my dream for a successful future. I now realize that it was God's abundant light that illuminated a pathway to finding balance and rest in a new season. Just thinking about entering the next chapter in life was so energizing and refreshing. I knew God was allowing me to come up for air and breathe! For this breakthrough in life, I am forever grateful!

After announcing my retirement, one of my colleagues asked if I felt afraid of retirement at this time in my life. My response to her was "No, I am not afraid because the Lord has given me the directive to retire, and I know He has great plans for me. I am walking by faith and believing God for the impossible dream. I know without a shadow of doubt that He will never leave me nor forsake me. I choose to trust God and will stand on His promises."

It is my hope that this young lady was able to see God's light shining through my response and message to her. Additionally, I pray that when I share testimonies with others, they will look beyond me and see the light of Jesus that shines in my life. Essentially, it's really not about me, but it's all about the One who lives inside of me.

To further extend this point, I must share another testimony. I recall a time when I presented a workshop to a group of high school teachers at the beginning of the school year. After my presentation, I remember the applause from the teachers and also positive comments that were verbally shared about the session.

As I was taking off my lapel microphone on stage, I remember an elderly gentleman walking up to me and saying, "Hello, Mrs. Small."

I immediately turned around and acknowledged him.

He said, "I really enjoyed your message today. I just want to say to you that if I don't see you again on this side of glory, I will see you on the other side."

He then shook my hand and walked away. Wow! What a compliment! I was totally speechless and could not even respond.

From all of the years that I have spoken at conferences, I had never heard this comment before. Thank God for allowing His glory to shine in my life and to touch the heart of a kind gentleman in the audience. This experience is a great reminder that as children of God, we must let the Father's light shine so that men may see Him at work in our lives not incidentally or every now and then. It must be an intentional, daily focus in our ministry walk that will lead others to Christ. With this said, I have decided to follow Jesus and experience the light of life. How about you?

Lessons Learned

Today I am more confident than ever that Jesus is the light of the world. If we follow Him, we will not have any need to fear darkness that surrounds us. Even though we experience cloudy days, lonely nights, sorrow, sickness, and various life challenges, we are yet walking in the supernatural light of the Father. Through His powerful light that never grows dim, we can find healing, deliverance, restoration, and peace. We know that the focus is not about us but about the One who shines within us. As we allow the Lord to shine through our testimonies, we will have an opportunity to lead others out of darkness and into His marvelous light.

Let Us Pray!

Lord Jesus,

Thank You for reminding us that You are the light of the world yesterday, today, and forevermore. Teach us to walk daily in Your abundant light that gives us a glimpse of Your everlasting peace, hope, and glory. Cause Your light to shine in our lives so that others may know and follow You. In Your powerful name, we pray. Amen.

Chapter 2

WALKING IN THE LIGHT
Jessica Small

Thy word is a lamp unto my
feet, a light unto my path.
—Psalm 119:105 NIV

Have you ever felt like you were in a dark season in your life
and no matter how hard you tried to see the light, things still
seemed dark? There are times in our lives when we may feel
lost, abandoned, alone, or simply stuck. The good news is it is
a temporary moment or feeling that with faith will eventually
pass. I am a firm believer in prayer. My mom has always said,
"Prayer changes things," and she's right. I can testify to it.

A few years ago, I was in a dark place in my life. I was
working at a middle school as a teacher and coach. As much
as I enjoyed doing both, I was extremely stressed. I had to
teach six classes a day in addition to coaching multiple sports.
So my typical work day lasted ten to twelve hours. Long story
short, I got very sick one night and had to go to the ER due
to internal bleeding. I was so scared because I rarely ever get
sick, and I knew this was a serious attack on my body. My
amazing doctor found three ulcers in my stomach due to tak-

ing lots of aspirin. (Side note: I took aspirin because I was having bad headaches almost every day when I coached.) I'll never forget what my doctor said to me: "Jessica, you need to find a better job that will not cause you to stress." He was absolutely right. I took his advice and did not renew my contract. I took a leap of faith and decided to trust God.

That summer, I didn't have any jobs lined up. When I resigned from my teaching position, I didn't understand why all this was happening to me. First, hospitalization. Then, no job. A good friend/mentor of mine suggested I revamp my prayer life.

I have to admit I wasn't praying like I should and I needed to trust God more. So what happened? Well, I applied for several jobs in education. I felt so discouraged because I had no prospects or interviews. God was teaching me a lesson on waiting and trusting Him. During the wait, I literally worked three jobs just to pay my monthly bills. God gave me a sense of humility throughout this season in my life, and I trusted Him at His word.

This was my dark place in life. I felt that God was punishing me when in actuality He was teaching me to give my situation to Him.

> Wait on the LORD; be strong and
> take heart and wait for the LORD. (Psalms
> 27:14 NIV)

A former colleague of mine gave me a note card with words of encouragement during this season, and I'll never forget it. It was a quote by Chuck Swindoll: "Refuse to slacken, surrender, or quit the path of obedience to God, no matter how intense the pressure." From this one quote, I have learned to lean on God and obey Him. To this day, I have improved in the area of trusting, waiting, and listening to God's word.

I'm sure you may be curious to know what happened after I walked through such a dark area of my life. God opened the door to an exciting job opportunity. I was offered a position to teach Early College High School for freshman students. I truly enjoyed teaching at the high school level because I was able to guide students for college and career readiness. Another perk of the job was being able to create lessons with a variety of resources. There was no set curriculum, which gave me flexibility. My students were always actively engaged throughout the school days, and we had lots of fun together. I taught them how to create a resume, type a professional letter to their professors, conduct college and career searches, and much more.

Working as an Early College High School instructor gave me a great feeling as I was able to impact the lives of many students. What a great feeling of accomplishment! God not only placed me in a less stressful environment but He allowed me to serve students with pleasure.

I received many kind appreciation letters from former students that I love to keep. Here are snippets of some of my favorite letters that always touch my heart whenever I read them:

> I always thought we were similar and
> we actually are. Being transparent is one
> of your best qualities, I aspire to be that
> way someday. You have goals and because

you envision what you want, I believe one day you will have everything you want. I'm very happy that I got to meet such a woman. All my best wishes to your future.

—Jeanette

Thank you so much for being an awesome teacher and always having my back in anything. God bless you!

—Katherine

Although you are a teacher, you are easy to talk to. You are a friend that can listen and help me in any situation. What I learned from you is although we go through hard situations, we just have to deal with it and do the best we can.

—Anthony

Anytime I need uplifting or encouragement, I go to my "They love me" files from previous years and enjoy reading special letters from my students. It always puts a smile on my face while I cry happy tears. With all the love and support, I decided to create a quilt with every letter I received from my awesome students. This quilt will not only keep my body warm but is a reminder that I am covered by the blood and blessed to lead great students in my classroom.

In summary, I thank God for His perfect timing. He is an on-time God! I didn't think I was going to get the Early College Instructor position, but God made a way. I love how God answers our prayers so clearly without any confusion. I am grateful that I serve a God who can do anything but fail. Once He opens a door, no man can shut it.

Lessons Learned

What lesson did I learn from this whole experience? I learned to always have faith and trust God through the good times and the not-so-good times. I learned to never give up on God and to enhance my prayer life by simply rebuilding my relationship with Christ. I am a witness that our God is awesome! Finally, I learned through any dark phase of my life, I always find answers to my problem as I walk in His light!

Let Us Pray!

Dear Heavenly Father,

I am so grateful for Your light that brightens my darkest days and clears my pathway to hope, change, and healing. Guide me through Your Holy Word and teach me to trust and walk in obedience to Your will. In Jesus's name! Amen.

Chapter 3

AMBASSADORS OF LIGHT

The night is nearly over; the
day is almost here. So let us put
aside the deeds of darkness and
put on the armor of light.
—Romans 13:12

One of the most exciting career opportunities that I have experienced is presenting professional development workshops for teachers and school administrators. I really enjoy sharing my personal stories from my lens as a classroom teacher during educational conferences as well. Whenever I am asked to speak at conferences, I often consider many details including the purpose, content, audience, location, what's going on in that particular community/organization, etc. One other important detail that I must think about is my wardrobe and what I will wear. Since I am a very detail-minded individual, I usually consider comfort, colors, jewelry, shoes, and the appropriate dress code for the occasion. While these are decisions that I must carefully make before I stand before my audience, I recognize that I must also consider my expressions and actions because they certainly speak louder than words. Basically, the outer garments are not as important as what's projected from within. What really matters is the message that I convey from my heart. The key question is am I projecting Christ as an ambassador of light?

Now that I am older and wiser, I have learned to be more intentional in my prayers before making decisions particularly before a speaking engagement. Today, I go to God in prayer asking for guidance on how to represent Him so that my work is pleasing in His sight. I now understand that representing Christ as an ambassador is more than the physical outlook—the matching jewelry, stylish shoes, and the pop colors to bring out the outfit. Rather it's more about the spiritual outlook and outcome of the message. I wholeheartedly agree with the old adage that reminds us that people are not interested in how much we know but rather how much we care. Essentially, I have discovered that even before the audience can hear my audible message, I must hear from God before I begin to speak for Him. The primary message that I hope to convey to others is that Jesus is the light of this dark world. In order to do this, I must first put on the armor of light so that others may see His image in my life.

As an ambassador for the Lord, I must shift my focus to what God is saying to His people in these last days. I pray that God will speak through me and allow others to see His peace, love, and grace at work through me. This is important and speaks volumes to any audience. When people are searching for answers or have a thirst for the truth, they are usually looking for individuals with a genuine smile, a love for helping others, and a caring spirit. These are areas that can be a source of light for believers and nonbelievers. So before I stand before any audience, I must enter my secret closet and ask God to use me as a vessel of light that will bring hope to a dark world during seasons of despair.

I recognize that people around the world have personal needs and problems in their lives that they may never share aloud. We never know who is sitting in an audience, who is sitting next to us on a plane or in church or in school, or even standing in the line at the grocery store. When people see God's light radiating through our lives, it provides a glimpse of hope, peace, and victory—a sense of winning or accomplishment. As ambassadors of light, we have an opportunity to be transparent vessels reflecting the light of God's goodness and love by sharing our life stories and testimonies.

I recall once speaking at a university to prospective teachers majoring in early childhood education. The auditorium was filled with men and women who had an interest in working with young children from infants and toddlers to second graders at the elementary school level. After concluding my keynote, I remember meeting several students who shared their passion with teaching and how they were inspired by my motivational message. There was one student who put his comments this way: "After hearing you speak today, I felt that I had heard a great sermon and I was waiting for someone to pass the offering plate." He also went on to say that he was planning to graduate in the spring and couldn't wait to work in a school teaching young children. This was certainly a powerful message of encouragement that I received in humility and thankfulness to God.

I praise the Father for allowing His light to shine and inspire a prospective teacher to continue his career journey for the sake of young children. This experience was a great reminder that we do not have to stand and tell others that we are believers or even wear a T-shirt that states our faith in God. We do not have to scream and shout to audiences to motivate them. Through our actions and messages from the heart, we can ignite a fire that will draw others to Christ. Essentially, we are indeed ambassadors of light and we stand as a city on a hill that cannot be hidden (Matthew 5:14). As we let our light shine daily, others will be able to see Jesus in our lives and will be compelled to follow Him.

As we reflect God's light in our daily lives, we must prepare for our ministry assignments by reading and studying God's Word. As we exercise this routine, we will be guided on the pathway of righteousness to be witnesses for the Lord. I am reminded in Psalm 119:105 that the Word of the Lord is a lamp unto our feet and a light unto our path. As we walk in this dark world, we must be careful to stay on the right path so that we do not stumble and fall. Yes, there are many distractions that we may encounter in life that could cause us to trip or fall by the wayside. And once we get off track and lose our directions in life, we often take detours that lead us into dark paths. This is a signal that we have lost sight of our spiritual compass which is God's Word.

One personal experience that comes to mind is when I have entered a very dark movie theater. Walking up steps and searching for your assigned seat in a large movie theater is often challenging particularly if the movie has already started. The floor lights are usually dim and do not provide sufficient light to get to one's destination. For example, if I leave the theater to purchase snacks while the movie is in progress, I often find myself searching aimlessly for my seat when I return.

I must share a secret I discovered for finding my seat whenever I need to leave and reenter the theater. It's not a magic formula, but it's as simple as looking up. I have learned to look up, scan the crowd, and try to find a glimpse of light in the darkness. Now this only works if my husband is sitting in the audience. When I look up, I can usually see Rudy's radiant silver hair shining in the darkness. This is my guiding light to my seat. Now whenever we go to a concert or a movie, I can easily get back to my seat by looking for a silver halo that actually glows even in the darkness. My husband calls this his crown of glory, and he wears it quite well!

What is my point in sharing this example? Many people are searching for answers and a light that will brighten their pathway during times of challenging storms and seasons of darkness. Sometimes people look for answers to their daily dilemmas in the wrong places and from the wrong sources. As ambassadors for Christ, we can lead others to the right source so that they can make it safely through life's storms. As we intentionally put on the armor of light and walk in God's image, we can lead others to repentance, healing, and a new life in Jesus Christ. Even without saying a word, we can let people witness the love of Christ through our daily actions. Just a smile could help make someone's day and bring a sense of hope. As I often tell teachers during workshops, a smile in any language is contagious, so let's be a carrier and spread it around.

Finally, let us put on the full armor of light in such dark and perilous times. We recognize that "our struggle is not against flesh and blood, but against the rulers, against the authorities, against the powers of this dark world and against the spiritual forces of evil in the heavenly realms" (Ephesians

6:12). With this in mind, my message to the world today is simply this: It's time to get dressed, obey God's Word, and allow our lives to reflect the love of Jesus Christ, our Lord. As we follow Jesus and stand on His promises, I believe we will experience victory on the battlefield of life. Let us collectively put on the armor of light while it is day so that the world may revere Christ as Savior and Lord. I have decided to follow Jesus who is the light of the world. How about you?

Lessons Learned

I have gained a greater understanding of my responsibility to put on the armor of light to cast off the darkness that is evident throughout the world. No, the armor is not just about the garments we wear on the outside, but more importantly, it's about what we reflect from the inside out. We must pause and ask ourselves, "Are we more concerned about pleasing the world, or do we focus on pleasing the Master? Are we dressing with a focus on our outward appearance, or is our primary focus on projecting Christ from our hearts?" These are important questions to consider as we seek to reflect the powerful and abundant light of Christ. I encourage each of us to shift our focus from the clothes we wear to the invitations we send from the heart to win souls for the Lord. What a great way to reflect God's love particularly in dark seasons! Let us continuously shine for Him!

Let Us Pray!

Father God,

We thank You for allowing us to be ambassadors of light in a very dark and sinful world. Teach us to stand tall as beacons of hope that will draw unbelievers to you before it is too late. Strengthen us to shine daily in our conversations, on our jobs, in our homes, communities, and throughout the land. Allow Your abundant light to spread like wildfire around the world so that others may receive You as their Savior. In Your matchless name, I pray. Amen.

Chapter 4

This Little Light of Mine

Jessica Small

Arise, shine, for your light has come,
and the glory of the Lord rises upon you.
—Isaiah 60:1 NIV

Nelson Mandela once said, "As we let our own light shine, we unconsciously give other people permission to do the same." This quote resonates with me in so many ways and is very true in my opinion. Each and every day, we have a choice to let our light shine no matter the circumstance or current situation. I believe if we shine through areas in our lives such as work, home, and community, it can help us persevere during dark phases and challenging times in our lives.

How do I let my light shine even in the rain? First things first, I've learned to have a positive reframe on every negative situation that I have and will encounter. Through life experiences, minor setbacks, bad news, and negative feedback, I decided to change my mindset on how I handle disappointments. This mindset has taken a lot of time and practice over the past few years, but it has helped me tremendously. For example, at work there were times when I didn't like my teacher evaluation and thought I deserved a higher score. God revealed to me that evaluations are not meant to be hurtful or condescending but simply provide feedback. God also showed me that evaluations are one's opinion of you but doesn't necessarily mean that you are all of those things that are stated. Once I realized this, it was easy for me to have a positive attitude about my future evaluations and any negative comment or situation.

I've found out that the best way for me to shine bright is by doing things that I really enjoy. I love helping others, and each day I ask God to show me how I can bless at least one person. I remember back in 2014, my former principal asked me to coordinate an all-girls conference for middle school-aged students. The conference was titled "She Matters," and the focus was on self-esteem, hygiene, leadership, and goal setting. This was an opportunity to *shine* in my career and utilize what God has called me to do, which is to serve others. I had speakers, engaging sessions for the girls, prizes, food, and most importantly fun. I was very pleased with the impact the conference made on the girls. Overall, it was a great turnout and success! I am truly thankful that my principal trusted me and appointed me to do something out of my comfort zone; it made a difference in more ways than one.

Letting my light shine at work has brought many great memories. However, when it comes to letting my light shine around family and friends, it is a different story. Personally, when I do experience darkness, I act like everything is going well in my life. I give the impression that everything is fine. But the people that really know me know when I'm going through a difficult time. So how do I let my light shine during this phase? I have learned the power of prayer and fasting. I have an amazing prayer partner. I call her Sweet Betty. She is a pastor's wife and a longtime family friend. I love her so much because she has been with me throughout my ups and downs since I was a young girl. Sweet Betty has been a blessing to me and my family for many years. I am glad I have her in my life, and she is always one phone call or text away. I think it is so important to have a prayer partner that we can connect with on a consistent basis. I am a firm believer in mental health and having a spiritual confidant.

When I was ready for a career change and job searching, I had to shift my attitude and prayer life. God humbled me to be obedient, listen to Him more, and trust his word and timing. I'll never forget when I was going through that rough season; I felt like giving up. Let me share a brief background story with you. It was the beginning of my eleventh year of teaching; and I was unhappy, frustrated, and bitter. I wanted out and was ready for a change. I applied for thousands of jobs (not kidding) and would only hear back via email that I didn't get the position. After constant disappointment e-mails, I had a conversation with my mom. She told me to stop applying for a while because it was causing me to stress and affecting my current work assignment. My mom is a big prayer warrior which has helped me throughout my life. Mom suggested that I start to pray and fast. I was praying at the time but not fasting. My mom also offered to pray and fast with me one day a week. I agreed to it. At first, I felt everything was still the same. But the key is to be consistent with our prayer and fast times, and so I continued. About three weeks passed, and everything was so different in my life. My attitude was better; I focused on making the most of where I was working and went above and beyond my work assignment. I owe it all to God because I couldn't have done any of this without Him. One day after work, on a Friday afternoon, I got a call about a great job opportunity and the company wanted to set up an interview with me. By the way, I applied for this job several months ago. I was so thrilled to get an interview that I began to cry. On this same day, I fasted. I immediately thanked *God* for the blessing. The interview went great, and God made it very smooth for me. There wasn't any question that I couldn't answer. I was ecstatic. After the interview, I felt good but wasn't sure if I was going to get the job. We are our own worst critics, and I was up against four other outstanding candidates. My prayer was simply, "Lord, if this position is for me, please open the door. If it isn't, please close the door. I trust You, and I thank You for getting me to this point. I'm grateful." I kept fasting one day a week because it was part of my regime at this point in my life, and I was gaining so much clarity. Weeks passed, and I hadn't heard any news from the company. One day, the job was heavy on my mind at work, and I decided to go pray in my office. That same day I was offered the position. I also fasted on this day. All glory to God! I accepted the position and resigned from teaching after almost eleven years. I enjoyed being an educator and have so many sweet memories that I will always cherish. Teaching will forever be my first love. It was bittersweet to leave the field of education and say goodbye to my students. In my heart, I knew this was all about God's perfect timing and was a part of His master plan. Praise God!

Lessons Learned

The main lesson I learned is to always go to God and seek to obey His will. He knows what's best for us and has every answer to our needs. I challenge each of you to make prayer and fasting a part of your life. You'll be amazed what God can do and will do. Another lesson that is very important to remember as we obey God's Word is to look in the mirror each morning and declare true commitment that we will shine for the Lord. I now like to sing the song "This Little Light of Mine, I'm Gonna Let It Shine" that I learned growing up in vacation Bible school. These words remind me to let my light shine daily in my home, school, work, and everywhere I go. More than ever before, I am determined to let it shine, let it shine, let it shine!

Let Us Pray!

Dear Heavenly Father,

Thank You for showing me how to let my light shine on a daily basis. Thank You for your grace and kindness. I always want to strive to be like You and allow others to see the Jesus in me. Please help me to remember each morning when I wake up to shine in everything I do. I give You all the honor and praise as I ask these things in Your great name! Amen.

Chapter 5

LET THERE BE LIGHT

And God said, "Let there be light,"
and there was light. God saw that
the light was good, and He separated
the light from the darkness.
—Genesis 1:3–4

The story of the creation is one of my favorite biblical passages that reminds me of God's great and supernatural power. To know that I serve a heavenly Father who can speak a few words and cause things to change is so amazing to me. Whenever I read Genesis chapter 1, I am totally in awe about God's sovereign authority to speak three words which began the creation of the heaven and the earth. Throughout the book of Genesis, we see many areas of God's great hand at work and how quickly things came into being just by the words "Let there be." There is no one else who has this source of power, and there is none like Him.

In Genesis 1:4, we see that God separated the light from the darkness and declared the light day and the darkness was called night. From the book of Genesis, I see God as an unusual artist with an eye for detail and purpose. Not only did God supernaturally separate the darkness from light but we know that He also created symbols of light that would shine forth even in darkness. When God hung the moon and stars in the sky, He painted a beautiful backdrop for the world to experience light even in the night. Additionally, we know that our Father created seasons that are evident during certain times of the year in various parts of the world. Each season reflects its own uniqueness and beauty and its own weather and seasonal changes in the earth. What an amazing addition to God's masterpiece and a great reflection of His omnipotent power, majesty, and glory!

As I consider each of the four seasons in the earth—fall, winter, spring, and summer—I have come to realize that each season also represents a particular time or experience in our lives. I have often heard faith-based leader's reference various seasons as storms in life. Essentially, there are three storm phases that one may encounter during life's journey:

1. Entering a storm
2. In the midst of a storm
3. Coming out of a storm

I must say that I have personally experienced each phase of a storm at some point in my life. The storms remind me of dark seasons in my life when I faced a challenge such as the loss of a loved one or friend, sickness, family challenges, transitions in life, work-related issues, financial losses, and the list goes on and on. As I walked in the midst of a storm in phase two, I usually experienced feelings of hopelessness and fear that I would never get through this phase. This season was indeed characterized by a critical time filled with deep despair and disappointment in life.

I can remember a challenging experience when I slipped into a period of depression following a major financial setback in my business. It was a very difficult season in my life that I had never encountered before. During this time frame, I felt I was walking through a valley experience all alone with no help in sight. While the enemy was speaking, "You will never make it out," in one ear, I could hear "Hold on" in the other ear. While I had a desire to hold on to God's promises in the midst of this storm, I remember the pain and burden that caused me to lose hope. As you read the words of my testimony, I hope that you will find encouragement to trust God in the midst of your personal storm just as I did. Although it was not an easy road to travel, I want to share my story so that you can see how God intervened and had the final say.

It all started in 2005 when I met with a contractor to discuss what I considered a business opportunity of a lifetime. From my lens, it appeared to be a dream come true. Not only would the contract offer a tremendous financial increase for my business but more importantly it would allow me to be a blessing to others. This was indeed an answer to my prayer, "Lord, bless me to be a blessing." I just knew I was on the road to success with God's favor in my view.

I was given a week to review my contract before actually signing the paperwork. Before the week ended, I received a call from the contractor who shared some startling news. The contractor explained that the company would not be able to follow through with the current contract as written due to budget constraints. Although the organization was willing to make a counter offer, it would be a major decrease in the initial contract amount. I was totally devastated as this news took me by surprise! It was as if my once-in-a-lifetime contract had become a shattered dream that would never come together again.

After hearing this disappointing news, my heart became heavy as I faced a great financial loss in my business. The pain became more unbearable each day as I tried to analyze what I had done wrong and why this was happening to me. The disappointment I experienced became so unbearable that it shifted me into a state of deep depression. I continuously tried to analyze the problem, but I could not shake the pain that escalated in my life. I now realize that I lost sight of God's promises and became distracted by my circumstances. Essentially, I allowed what appeared to be a hopeless situation to overshadow my faith which left me feeling totally defeated and emotionally destroyed.

For the next six weeks, I grew deeper and deeper into a cloud of darkness. During this time, I experienced several losses: a loss of appetite, weight, sleep, and the desire for activities I enjoyed in the past. For example, I usually loved to go out to enjoy meals with my family and friends. However, during this stage of deep depression, I had no desire to eat out or even eat meals at home. Not only did I feel sick daily, I started to look the part as well. I had lost my appetite for living during this phase of my stormy season.

I had very little interaction with my children, and they would often ask, "What's wrong, Mom?" It was very hard to express my feelings, so I would try to tune out any questions. I no longer enjoyed connecting with my family, and conversations were very limited during this period in my life. I literally had reached a point of disconnection with others as

I shifted my focus from fighting for my life to fighting what appeared to be a losing battle.

During the day, I would often curl up on the floor in a fetal position looking for comfort. It was very difficult falling asleep at night, and once I was able to sleep, I would begin to dream. For several nights, I dreamt that I was drowning in a large body of water. Darkness was everywhere and I felt I was sinking in a black sea of hopelessness. The interesting thing was that as I was slowly sinking, I never touched the bottom of the sea. In essence, what I experienced each night was an endless drowning where I could not see anyone to help or rescue me. It was indeed a dark setting where I looked diligently for a glimpse of light but could not find it.

One day, a dear friend called and said her daughter had invited her to attend a Women's Encounter the following weekend. I remember her specifically saying to me that while her daughter was praying one morning, the Lord spoke to her and said invite Cynthia Small. At the time, I did not feel like traveling nor connecting with people so I declined the invitation. I had decided to send my daughter instead. My husband strongly encouraged me to attend the service, but I had no intention of going anywhere. It became clear that I was slipping into a time of self-pity where I really felt there was no help in store for me.

Later that night after falling asleep, I dreamt I was once again sinking into a deep dark sea. But this time, I noticed something different happening that I had not seen before. While I was sinking, I looked up and saw a glimpse of light. I also saw a hand reaching out to help me. When I clutched the hand in my dream, I could actually feel large chains beginning to break around my neck. Suddenly, I saw light all around me and could finally breathe again. What a refreshing experience even in my dream!

When I woke up, I felt I had received a special message from the Lord. I shared the dream with my husband and told him that I would plan to attend the Women's Encounter after all. Of course my husband was thrilled to hear this news. He proceeded to help me pack for the trip and made the travel arrangements without any hesitation. Peace was certainly restored in our house that day as we both were now on the same page. Could it be that we both began to see a glimpse of light in my darkest hour?

The next day while flying to the Women's Encounter, I began to feel sick to my stomach and wanted to return home. But God gave me strength to carry on. I now understand that the enemy tried to create roadblocks to keep me from attending the Women's Encounter so that I would not receive what God had in store for me. But even before I arrived at the church, I began to tell God thank you for the plans He had just for me. I had learned not to wait until the battle was over, but to rejoice and dance in advance.

When I arrived at the church, I could hear the praise and worship service in progress. Although I was physically weak, I was excited to be with other believers in the house of the Lord. I did not care how I looked and walked passed a mirror in the lobby so that I could get to my seat in the sanctuary. I was no longer concerned about my appearance of significant weight loss, clothing that didn't fit, and fatigue that was evident as I walked into the service. What I know for sure is that I was desperate to find Jesus. I began to think if I can just get to the altar, perhaps I can get a breakthrough.

Finally, the worship leader called for women who were in need of prayer. I could not wait to get to the altar and did not care who saw me or what they thought of me. I had reached a point of desperation where I knew I needed a touch from the Lord. As I walked down the aisle, I asked God to show the prayer warriors my condition and what I was going through. I did not feel I had the energy to explain my issues, so I asked the Lord to let it be revealed.

As I approached one of the prayer leaders at the altar, she held her hands out to me and smiled. Right away she began to read me like a book. She whispered things like, "I see that you have worked in children's ministry with young people, but you have lost your desire for ministry work. I also see that you have a family with children, but you are not spending time with them as you would like." Finally, the missionary said to me, "Daughter, the Lord has seen your tears. You have lost your joy, but tonight you will get your joy back." The last thing I remember the missionary saying is "Father in the name of Jesus." The Lord stepped in and took the lead from there. Father God met me in a supernatural way at the Women's Encounter; and that night I was healed, delivered, and set free. Indeed the Lord spoke light into my dark experience of depression and restored my joy, peace, appetite, and the desire to work in His vineyard once again.

Although the enemy desired to steal, kill, and destroy my life's dreams, the Lord spoke life and that more abundantly (John 10:10). What I received from the Lord far outweighed the financial losses I previously experienced. Indeed the Lord shifted my focus from the desire for material gain to a focus on eternal gain. Essentially, I began to spiritually see that God had allowed this door to close so that He could share greater plans for me to prosper just as He promised (Jeremiah 29:11).

I praise God for taking me through this period of affliction so that I could learn His statutes (Psalm 119:71) and stand on His promises. Today I yet walk in victory sharing God's abundant light through my personal testimony. It is my hope that when others listen to my struggle with depression and how the Lord set me free, they too will desire to have an encounter with the Lord. I pray that souls will begin to experience a hunger for the Lord and a thirst for His righteousness in these perilous times. While the world is searching for answers in dark seasons, I believe that God is yet speaking "Let there be light" even today. No matter how challenging your stormy seasons become, I encourage you to trust God and watch Him bring you out of darkness into His abundant light. Just as the Lord spoke light into my dark situation, He can surely do the same for you!

As we continue our journey, I must share another testimony concerning a different kind of storm. It all started as a goal that my husband and I shared even before we were married. It was our desire to have a child of our own someday, and we prayed faithfully that our Father would honor this request. During the first few years of our marriage, we visited doctors who would either offer suggestions that involved taking infertility drugs, having surgery, or looking at the adoption process. Neither of these recommendations appealed to us. But after looking for answers from the medical profession, it seemed that we were walking down a dead-end street. Finally, one day my husband said to me, "Maybe we should go ahead and look at adopting a child." Somehow I kept thinking surely there is a better option for us. Indeed God had a plan with our name on it. We just didn't see it at the time.

I recall going to church one Friday night to attend a revival. This was the last night of the weeklong event, and I did not want to miss it. I felt that I really needed to hear an encouraging word from the Lord. As I sat in the service, I was indeed encouraged and energized to continue to trust God for our miracle blessing. Before the service ended, the evangelist asked everyone who wanted something special from God to form a line in the nearest aisle. We were asked to let God know our needs and individual requests. It was at that point in the service that I decided to trust God and ask Him for a child. Yes, I had made this appeal before; but this time, it was an intentional request followed by intentional faith. I silently prayed a bold prayer by simply saying, "Lord, I just want a child of my own."

Fast forward, six weeks later, I began to feel really tired in my body and made an appointment to see my doctor. The doctor ordered several tests for me so that he could rule out a few things based on my medical history. After the tests were completed, I was released to go home and rest. The doctor's office would contact me with the test results later that afternoon.

Needless to say, I was curious to hear the results and waited with great anticipation for the call. Later that afternoon, the phone rang, and it was the nurse. I took a deep breath as I anxiously listened for the test results. Then I heard three words I had always hoped to hear. The nurse said to me, "Mrs. Small, we have reviewed your tests, and I have good news for you. The tests show that you are pregnant!"

I began to cry and rejoice in the Lord and the nurse began to cry along with me. She was aware of the waiting period that we had experienced while praying for a child of our own. This was certainly a dream come true and a miraculous answer to our prayers. The Lord spoke, "Let there be light," into a season of darkness for us. Through God's supernatural radiation of light, we were blessed with the gift of a healthy baby boy in the months ahead.

But that's not the end of the story! Remember I had asked the Lord for one child when I stood in the prayer line at the revival. Well we later discovered that God was not finished with our family and had another plan in mind. Three years later, almighty God spoke twice and blessed us with healthy twins. So God granted us a total of three miracle babies. I call them our "trinity blessings"—one for the Father, one for the Son, and one for the Holy Spirit. Each of our children were born full term, healthy, and full of life. Praise God for His gift of precious children! (Psalm 127:3). We yet magnify the Lord for our miracle blessings—Jay, Jessica, and Jason! For this reason, I am encouraged to project God's abundant light as I share this testimony with others. Since we overcome by the words of our testimony (Revelation 12:11), it is an honor to continuously share my story for His glory!

Lessons Learned

I have learned to trust and lean on the Lord during the darkest times of my life. I know for sure that if we learn to wait on God and trust his timing, He will answer our prayers. It has become crystal clear to me that no matter where I go or whatever challenges I encounter in life, He is always there with me.

I now see the light and understand what David meant when he wrote,

> Where can I go from your spirit? Where can I flee from your presence? If I ascend to the heavens, you are there. If I make my bed in hell, behold you are there. If I take the wings of the morning and dwell in the uttermost parts of the sea, even there your hand shall lead me and your right hand shall hold me. (Psalm 139:7–10)

Finally, when God speaks, "Let there be," I have learned to stand on God's promises and watch adverse winds shift in my favor. I now rest in knowing that God is able to speak light over darkness, life over death, peace over confusion, and healing over disease. When God speaks the words "Let there be light," we know by faith that it shall be done!

Let Us Pray!

> Most gracious Father,
>
> Thank You for revealing Your miraculous power through Your abundant light. Strengthen us to stand in faith and trust You as we encounter valley experiences in our lives. Help us to recognize Your goodness and new mercies that are evident each morning. You are such a faithful God in whom we praise, honor, and give all the glory. For Thine is the kingdom, the power, and the glory forever. Amen.

Chapter 6

THE GREEN LIGHTS OF LIFE

Do not gloat over me, my enemy!
Though I have fallen, I will
rise. Though I sit in darkness,
the Lord will be my light.
                        —Micah 7:8

Have you ever been able to drive through a number of inter-sections and the traffic light was green? Whenever this occurs for me, I am amazed and grateful to make green lights instead of stopping at every block for a red light. Even on days when I have been trying to get to an appointment during rush hour, I know that God is the only one who can make provisions for me to arrive at my destination safely and on time. During these instances, I recognize that God had encamped His angels around me and that He kept me from accidents, delays and dark situations that could have been fatal. But God in His infinite and unmerited grace allowed His light to shine and serve as my refuge during dangers seen and unseen as I traveled to various locations on the earthly highway. For these moments of grace, I am so grateful.

Not only have I experienced the favor of God on the highways of life but God has also been with me when flying to various conferences and speaking engagements. I vividly recall times when I boarded the plane thinking I would be able to take off as scheduled. There were several occasions when that did not happen. The Lord has reminded me before I get on a plane to always pray for a safe journey. As I take my first step on the airplane, I intentionally lay my right hand on the plane and specifically ask for traveling grace not only for me and my family but for everyone on the plane. I pray intentionally for the pilots and ask the Lord to give them wisdom to make the right decisions as they navigate the aircraft. Before I get to my seat, I walk in confidence knowing that God is in control and will guide those of us on the plane safely to our final destination.

I recall a time when I was in Los Angeles waiting for the plane which was delayed in another city due to inclement weather. Each half hour, the airline agent would announce the flight has been further delayed. Needless to say, I was tired, hungry, and so ready to return home. After waiting for three hours at the airport, our plane finally arrived. Although it was almost midnight, I was just happy to be able to finally head home. As we were about to board the plane, I remember a couple introducing themselves and letting me know that they had attended the same conference that I just attended in Los Angeles. We began to talk, and when I entered the plane, I was distracted and did not pray or lay my right hand on the plane. I did not even realize this until I noticed that we had been sitting at the gate for more than thirty minutes. I remember hearing that there was a malfunction in the landing gear and that it needed to be checked out. Then about twenty minutes later, the pilot said the tires needed to be checked as well. As we sat on the plane, the air flowing was not cool, and it began to feel very uncomfortable and quite warm. I began to ask the Lord to show the airline crew what to do so that we could push back from the gate and head home.

The Holy Spirit spoke softly and reminded me, *You did not pray before you entered the plane as you have done in the past.* I quickly repented and told the Lord how sorry I was. I remembered that I had been distracted, but this was not an excuse. Feeling guilty for the delay for the other passengers on board, I laid my right hand on the side of the window and prayed for safety, traveling grace, and for God to correct any malfunctioning equipment before we left the airport. Within minutes, the lights begin to flicker on the plane. The cool air began to flow, and I could hear the captain saying that all systems had been checked and for everyone to prepare for takeoff. Hallelujah to almighty God for His faithfulness and awesome power!

The flight home was very smooth, and we were able to land safely in Dallas in just a few hours. I shared this experience with my husband when I arrived at the baggage claim area. This was another green light testimony that I could not wait to share. My husband was happy to hear the good news of God's miraculous timing and response to prayer. He also went on to remind me that my testimony sounded similar to the story of Jonah when he was tossed into the sea during the storm. Humorously, my husband said, "It's a wonder that the passengers didn't throw you off the plane." For about a week, he called me Jonah's friend. Now whenever we travel on flights together, he reminds me to be obedient and lay hands on the plane as we enter the aircraft. We both believe in the power of prayer and travel by faith knowing that God is our green light to our earthly destinations and more importantly to our eternal home in glory!

I must share another green light story that I hope will bless someone reading this passage. On January 20, 2018, my husband and I were involved in a car accident as we traveled to have dinner at one of our favorite restaurants. We were about to turn into the parking lot of the restaurant when we were suddenly hit from the rear by a drunk driver. Upon impact, I recall being pushed into another lane and spinning out of control. My immediate response was, "Oh, God!" It's interesting that I did not call my husband's name, my mom, dad, my pastor, sister, or brother; but I called on the Father.

The Lord covered us that night when we entered this storm that could have been fatal, but God said *no*. As we were spinning, we did not know where the car would stop. There were several trees on the side of the road. We could have hit one of them, but God encamped His angels about us and allowed the car to line up next to a huge tree rather than collide into it. There were a few witnesses who saw the entire accident, and ambulances and police quickly came to the scene.

I remember one of the witnesses running to the truck as soon as we were able to stop. He opened the door and asked if we were okay. He stayed with us and talked to us and let us know he had seen the accident and would give a complete report to police when they arrived. He was so kind and actually stayed with us until the paramedics came to check us out. I call him our guardian angel on the scene. When the paramedics arrived, we were able to walk slowly to the ambulance with assistance and were grateful that we were alert and were not carried on a stretcher to the hospital. I know that God was shining on us that dark night in our life and that He allowed us to experience the green light of life as we walked away without scratches—just sore muscles. Praise our God!

Fast forward, my husband and I participated in physical therapy for about eight weeks. We attended therapy sessions four days per week. This meant I would work half days and then go to therapy in the afternoon. Since my husband was retired, this did not present a challenge for him in scheduling visits. The good news is that we were able to attend therapy appointments together and help each other through this phase of recovery. While the therapy and medications helped ease our pains, we know that it was God who healed our bodies. What the enemy meant for evil, God almighty turned it around for our good. We continue to give Him praise for His healing touch and mighty hand of deliverance!

Once we were released from physical therapy, the insurance company began to process the claim and settlement from the accident. During this period, I began to reflect back on what God had done for us. One night when I was alone in the kitchen, I asked the Lord what the accident meant and what was I to learn from it. The Lord spoke these words to me: *I am preparing you for ministry. When you were hit from behind, you were being pushed into a new level of ministry.* I stopped and began to give God praise then and there in our kitchen. I did not ask what God wanted me to do at the time but just responded, "Yes, Lord," to His directive.

A few days later, the Lord prompted me to look at seminary classes to prepare for ministry work. Once I found the one I felt would prepare me for next steps in ministry, I inquired about the costs. When I received the total amount to complete seminary classes, I began to feel discouraged because we did not have the funds available for me to enroll at the time. My husband and I began to discuss different options to pay for the classes and even called to ask the dean about different financial options. In the meantime, the Lord spoke to me and said, *I am preparing you for ministry. Trust me.*

A few weeks later, I received a call from the insurance company handling our claim and was offered more than the total cost of the seminary classes. Praise God for His wondrous and miraculous acts of kindness. He is certainly an on-time God! I was able to enroll and pay for the classes up front and began that summer preparing for ministry. Once again, God gave us the green light that signaled for me to go forward in ministry and do greater works for His kingdom. Not only did the Lord bless me with the funds for seminary but he allowed me to complete the coursework in less than two years. Since I have graduated from seminary, the Lord has opened many doors for me to walk in my calling for His purpose. I continue to stand on His promises and know that only God can open doors that no man can shut (Revelations 3:8).

I recognize that it is time for God's people to be about His business. We must learn to reflect His light in today's dark world and stay on the battlefield of life in these perilous times. To further expound on this thought, I'd like to share an excerpt from a poem I've written that speaks to the importance of walking in our assignments and working while it is day.

Faithful Servants: On Business for the King

Faithful servants rise up and stand
As witnesses for Christ who believe and
   know,
That God has a plan and purpose
For His servants to work and spiritually
   grow.

We must work the work of Him that
   sent us
In fear and humility lest we boast,
Teaching and baptizing all nations
In the name of the Father, Son, and Holy
   Ghost.

It is now time for God's servants to recognize
That we must work while it is day,
For we know not the minute or the hour
When Christ shall return and call us away.

Let us go forth as chosen vessels
Sharing the peace that only God can bring,
Faithfully accepting the challenge to work
As anointed servants on business for the
   King.

(Excerpts from Pocketbook Praise, 2010)

Lessons Learned

I have discovered from challenging life experiences that God has a plan for each of us. Whatever He says to us, we must obey and follow His will. No matter what it looks like, sounds like, or feels like, we must trust God and His holy Word. Finally, we must stay in faith and know that God has called each of us to walk in a ministry assignment according to His purpose and divine plan. This means it's time to shift our focus from our problems to standing on God's promises. As we travel along life's journey, our Father will be our protection and guide. I know without a doubt that He will lead us and give us a way of escape through the green light of life.

Let Us Pray!

Father God,

Thank You for reminding us to walk in Your light even though the enemy paints a dark pathway in our lives. Help us to recognize that You are the Savior and light of the world and that nothing is impossible for You. Thank You for giving us the assurance that You are a guiding light and lamp unto our feet that lights our path. Help us to walk in Your abundant light that covers and keeps us safe in an unsafe world. Teach us to trust that You are the green light that will lead us to higher heights as we travel the highway to heaven. In your name, we pray. Amen.

Chapter 7

CLOSING HIGHLIGHTS

As we conclude our discussion and approach the final segment of this book, we hope that you have received words of encouragement and discovered a glimpse of hope for brighter days ahead. Please know that this is not the end of our stories but is only a taste of God's goodness found in His abundant light. We hope that this book is a timely and relevant resource that will bring light to dark situations that cast a shadow of despair in our homes, marriages, family finances, health, careers, and in our relationships with friends and loved ones. We know that in these perilous times, we need a source of light to help us survive the many challenges we face in life. We know now more than ever that we need God's light to shine today in the White House, the church house, the courthouse, the school house, and in our house daily. If we are to thrive and grow as children of light, we must first accept Jesus as the light of the world. Secondly, it is our responsibility to let His light shine in our lives that others may see Him through us. And finally, we must project a light that radiates through our actions, words, and deeds so that we may lead others to Christ—our Savior and King.

One of the major points emphasized throughout this book is that God is a powerful light even in a world of darkness. And even though we may wonder if we will ever see the breaking of day or light at the end of the tunnel, we must never give up or throw in the towel. We must sharpen our focus on God's abundant light through His Holy Word which is a "lamp unto our feet and a light unto our path" (Psalm 119:105). Let us hold on to God's promises which are designed to give us a sense of hope and peace during dark seasons in our lives. As we enter stormy experiences in life, let us remember that our God, Emmanuel, is with us. He will never leave us nor forsake us. His light is everlasting and never grows dim.

Finally, let us remember to keep our focus on the One who can speak peace in the midst of storms, joy in seasons of sorrow, strength in times of weakness, and victory over the attacks of the enemy. Nothing is impossible or too hard for our God. Jessica and I are both witnesses that God can do exceeding abundantly more than we could ever ask or think. As His servants and children of light, let us roll up our sleeves and begin to fulfill our assignments for the King. There is no need to worry or be afraid. Just remember we are under the witness protection plan that never expires.

This plan guarantees that no weapon formed against us shall prosper and that God is our refuge and strength, a very present help in times of trouble. Our Father has sent protection for each of us as we let our lights shine before men, women, boys, and girls. As ambassadors of light, we have been assigned two body guards—their names are Goodness and Mercy. Surely goodness and mercy shall follow us all the days of our lives, and we shall dwell in the house of the Lord forever (Psalm 23:6). Continue to be about our Father's business and know that you are covered by God's promises in His holy word.

As we conclude this learning journey, we'd like to leave a few ideas for allowing God's abundant light to shine brightly in your daily walk with the Father. May the following ideas in the appendix section serve as a springboard for walking intentionally as ambassadors of light. In these last days, we each have an assignment and must be about our Father's business. Now is the time for each of us to rise and shine, to encourage the hearts of others, and most importantly lead lost souls to Christ. Let us continuously reflect the love of our Savior by allowing our lights to radiate all over the world. We are confident that as we shine together, we can advance the kingdom and make God smile.

Let us connect today as beacons of light from the north, south, east, and west to spread the message that Jesus is the light of the world. Go forward and shine in His holy name!

APPENDIX

Appendix A

EMERGENCY LIGHTS

During a stormy season in life, turn on your emergency lights!
Meditate on God's Word and allow Him
to bring *light* in times of darkness.

When you are frightened and living in fear:

> Have I not commanded you? Be
> strong and courageous. Do not be afraid;
> do not be discouraged, for the Lord your
> God will be with you wherever you go.
> (Joshua 1:9)

When you are troubled and in despair:

> Do not let your hearts be troubled.
> You believe in God; believe also in me.
> (John 14:1)

When there is chaos all around you:

> We are hard pressed on every side,
> but not crushed; perplexed, but not

in despair; persecuted, but not abandoned; struck down, but not destroyed. (2 Corinthians 4:8–9)

When you need an answer to a problem:

Ask and it will be given to you; seek and you will find; knock and the door will be opened to you. (Matthew 7:7)

When you are anxious:

Do not be anxious about anything, but in every situation, by prayer and petition, with thanksgiving, present your requests to God. And the peace of God, which transcends all understanding, will guard your hearts and your minds in Christ Jesus. (Philippians 4:6–7)

When you feel the enemy is after you:

Whoever dwells in the shelter of the Most High will rest in the shadow of the Almighty. (Psalm 91:1)

When you feel discouraged:

Wait for the Lord; be strong and take heart and wait for the Lord. (Psalm 27:14)

When you need direction in life:

> Your word is a lamp for my feet, a light on my path. (Psalm 119:105)

When you feel like giving up:

> But those who hope in the Lord will renew their strength. They will soar on wings like eagles; they will run and not grow weary, they will walk and not be faint. (Isaiah 40:31)

When you are in the midst of the storm:

> God is our refuge and strength, an ever-present help in trouble. (Psalm 46:1)

When the enemy tells you that you can't make it:

> Therefore, my dear brothers and sisters, stand firm. Let nothing move you. Always give yourselves fully to the work of the Lord, because you know that your labor in the Lord is not in vain. (1 Corinthians 15:58)

When you feel tired and need rest:

> Come to me, all you who are weary and burdened, and I will give you rest. Take my yoke upon you and learn from me, for I am gentle and humble in heart,

and you will find rest for your souls. For my yoke is easy and my burden is light. (Matthew 11:28–30)

When you are in a dark place in life:

Do not gloat over me, my enemy! Though I have fallen, I will rise. Though I sit in darkness, the Lord will be my light. (Micah 7:8)

When you are bereaved and in mourning:

Blessed are those who mourn, for they will be comforted. (Matthew 5:4)

When you suffer afflictions:

The righteous person may have many troubles, but the Lord delivers him from them all. (Psalm 34:19)

When you can't sleep:

In peace I will lie down and sleep, for you alone, Lord, make me dwell in safety. (Psalm 4:8)

When you face life's storms and can't see a way out:

When you pass through the waters, I will be with you; and when you pass through the rivers, they will not sweep over you. When you walk through the fire, you will not be burned; the flames will not set you ablaze. (Isaiah 43:2)

When you need protection in times of trouble:

The name of the Lord is a fortified tower; the righteous run to it and are safe. (Proverbs 18:10)

When the enemy says you can't:

I can do all things through Christ who gives me strength. (Philippians 4:13)

When you are in need of a miracle or special blessing:

This is the confidence we have in approaching God: that if we ask anything according to his will, he hears us. And if we know that he hears us—whatever we ask—we know that we have what we asked of him. (1 John 5:14–15)

When you experience the fear of death and feel you can't make it in life:

Even though I walk through the darkest valley, I will fear no evil for you are with me; your rod and your staff, they comfort me. (Psalm 23:4)

When you feel defeated and unsuccessful in life:

> Keep this Book of the Law always on your lips; meditate on it day and night, so that you may be careful to do everything written in it. Then you will be prosperous and successful. (Joshua 1:8)

When doors have been closed in your face:

> I know your deeds. See, I have placed before you an open door that no one can shut. I know that you have little strength, yet you have kept my word and have not denied my name. (Revelations 3:8)

When someone has treated you unfairly:

> Do not repay anyone evil for evil. Be careful to do what is right in the eyes of everyone. (Romans 12:17)

When you think your dreams will never come true:

> Being confident of this, that he who began a good work in you will carry it on to completion until the day of Christ Jesus. (Philippians 1:6)

*Each scripture listed is from the New International Version (NIV) Bible.

Appendix B

RISE AND SHINE

Ten Ways to Spread Sunshine on a Cloudy Day

1. Pay for the meal or groceries of someone who is in line behind or in front of you.
2. Present a food gift card to someone living on the street or who needs a helping hand.
3. Share a smile! Remember: smiles are contagious and will help make someone's day.
4. Mail someone a "just thinking about you" card.
5. Let someone who has less grocery items than you go ahead of you in the checkout line.
6. Encourage someone with an affirmation, compliment, hug, high five, etc.
7. Write a note of encouragement to others. Place a note for children in their lunchbox or backpack. For adults, leave the note on their desk, in their mailbox, or on the breakfast table.
8. Pick up the phone and give someone a call just to share a word of encouragement.
9. Offer to pick up and/or deliver grocery items for a neighbor or senior citizen in your community.

10. Speak daily affirmations to encourage yourself in the Lord. To encourage someone else, change the word *I* to *You* or *mine* to *yours* in the sentences below. Declare positive affirmations to build up others when they are feeling down. Let it shine!

- o   I can do all things through Christ.
- o   I am fearfully and wonderfully made.
- o   I am the apple of God's eye.
- o   The battle is not mine, it's the Lord's.
- o   By His stripes, I am healed.
- o   I am productive and prosperous.
- o   I am awesome and amazing.
- o   I will conquer the day.
- o   I am focused on the positives today.
- o   I am somebody trying to tell everybody that they are somebody too!

Let your light shine before
others, that they may see
your good deeds and glorify
your Father in heaven.
— Matthew 5:16

We would love to hear from you!

Please contact us:

Family Dimensions, Inc.
P. O. Box 112362
Carrollton, TX 75006

Or email us:
cyndismall07@gmail.com
jessicalorensmall@gmail.com

Special thanks to the following people for providing a guiding light to this project:

Jo Wilsford
Mary Wallace
Cynthia Ridge

About the Authors

Jessica Loren Small and Dr. Cynthia Jackson Small

Dr. Cynthia Jackson Small is a certified family life educator, motivational speaker, and author who shares messages of hope through her teaching ministry. As the executive director and founder of Family Dimensions Inc., Cynthia provides consulting services to school districts, churches, and business communities. Her mission is to inspire and touch the lives of families and children worldwide so that they may thrive and grow one day at a time. After serving as the executive youth director at her church for twenty-seven years, Cynthia yet has a passion for children's ministries today. She also enjoys bowling, tennis, and spending time with her family. Dr. Small and her husband, Rudy, reside in Texas and are blessed with three miracle gifts from God—Jamaad, Jason, and Jessica.

Jessica Loren Small currently serves as an agent for Texas A&M AgriLife Extension Service and formerly worked as a college professor and middle school teacher in the North Texas area. Jessica holds a master's degree in kinesiology and enjoys sharing nutritional and physical fitness resources that will help individuals make healthy choices. In her spare time, she loves photography, watching movies, yoga, cycling, and traveling with her twin brother, Jason. With a passion for health and wellness, Jessica's goal is to let her light shine so that others may develop healthy lifestyles that will be pleasing and acceptable to God.